Tony Millionaire's
SOCK MONKEY™

Tony Millionaire's

SOCK MONKEY™

THE GLASS DOORKNOB

Ferndale Public Library
222 East Nine Mile Rd.
Ferndale, MI 48220
www.ferndale.lib.mi.us

DARK HORSE MAVERICK™

for

Becky

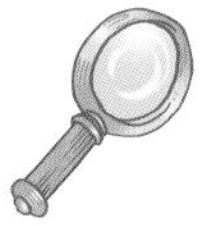

designer *Lia Ribacchi*
art director *Cary Grazzini*
editor *Philip D. Amara*
publisher *Mike Richardson*

published by
Dark Horse Comics, Inc.
10956 S.E. Main Street
Milwaukie, OR 97222

www.darkhorse.com
www.maakies.com

To find a comics shop in your area,
call the Comic Shop Locator Service
toll-free at 1-888-266-4226

First edition: September 2002
ISBN: 1-56971-782-6

1 3 5 7 9 10 8 6 4 2
PRINTED IN CHINA

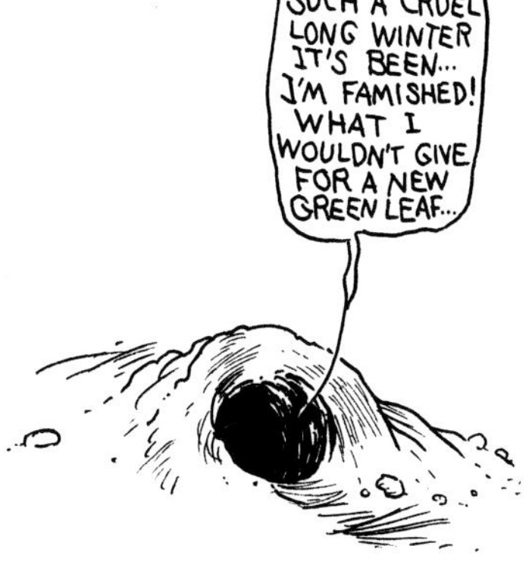
SUCH A CRUEL LONG WINTER IT'S BEEN... I'M FAMISHED! WHAT I WOULDN'T GIVE FOR A NEW GREEN LEAF...

ONE fine spring morning the Sock Monkey's friends clambered upstairs.

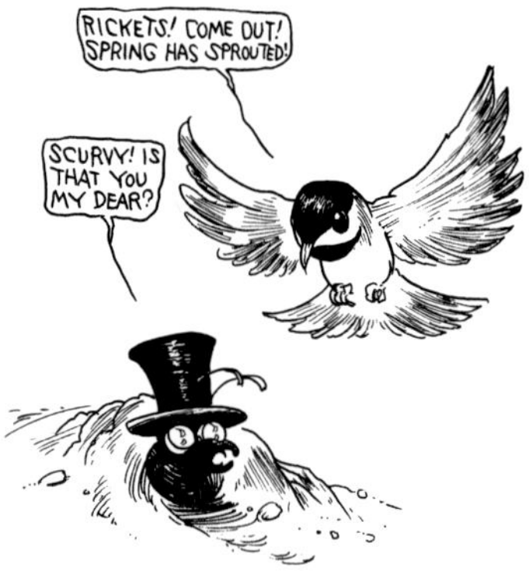
RICKETS! COME OUT! SPRING HAS SPROUTED!
SCURVY! IS THAT YOU MY DEAR?

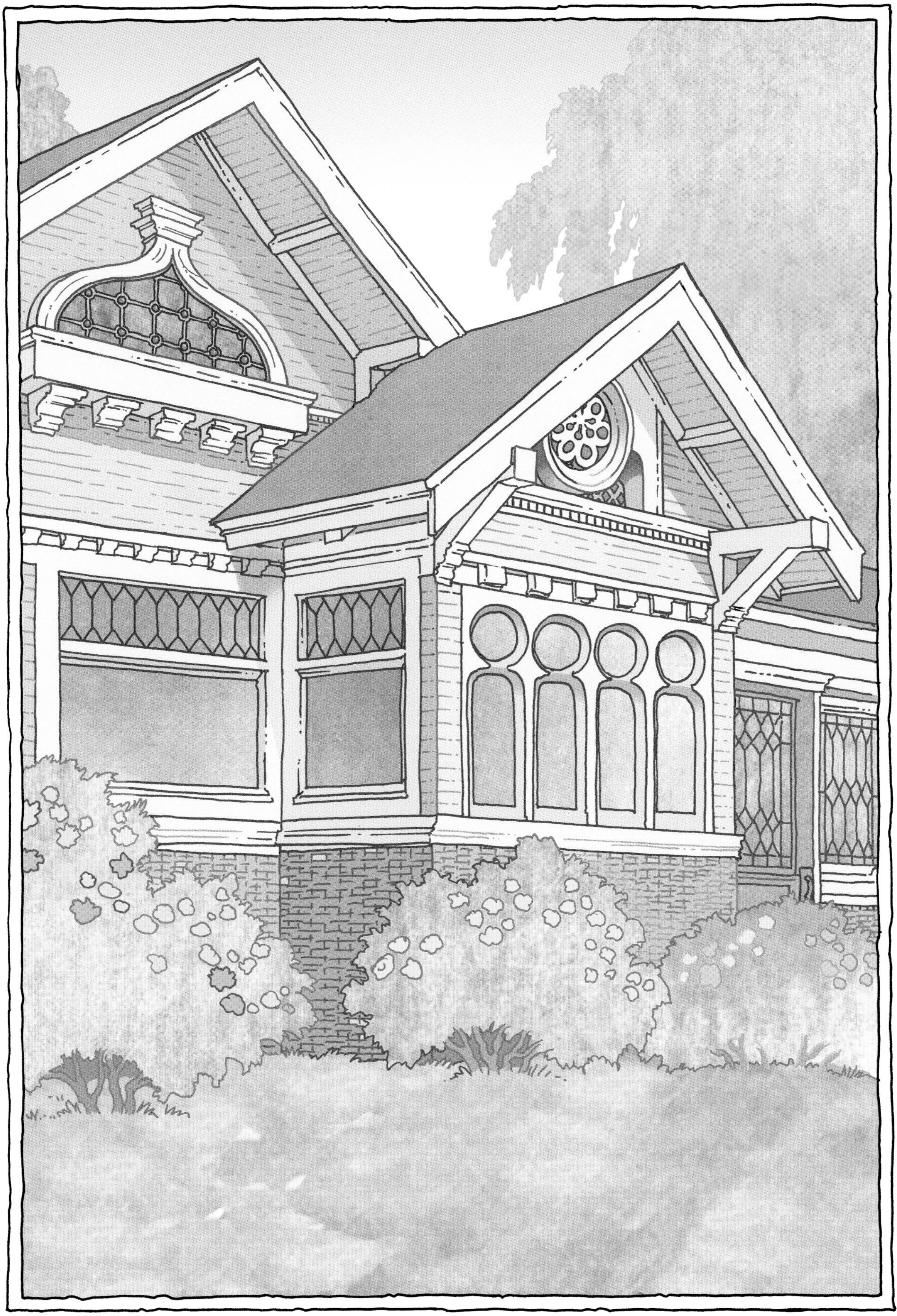

"WAKE up!" cried the crow, "Come see what Stormy found!"

"I found it too!" squeaked Inches.

Stormy spoke in his rumbling voice, "Hop onto my back and I'll give you a ride downstairs."

YES RICKETS, YOU'VE SLEPT LONG ENOUGH! WHY, YOU'RE MISSING THE WHOLE FEAST!

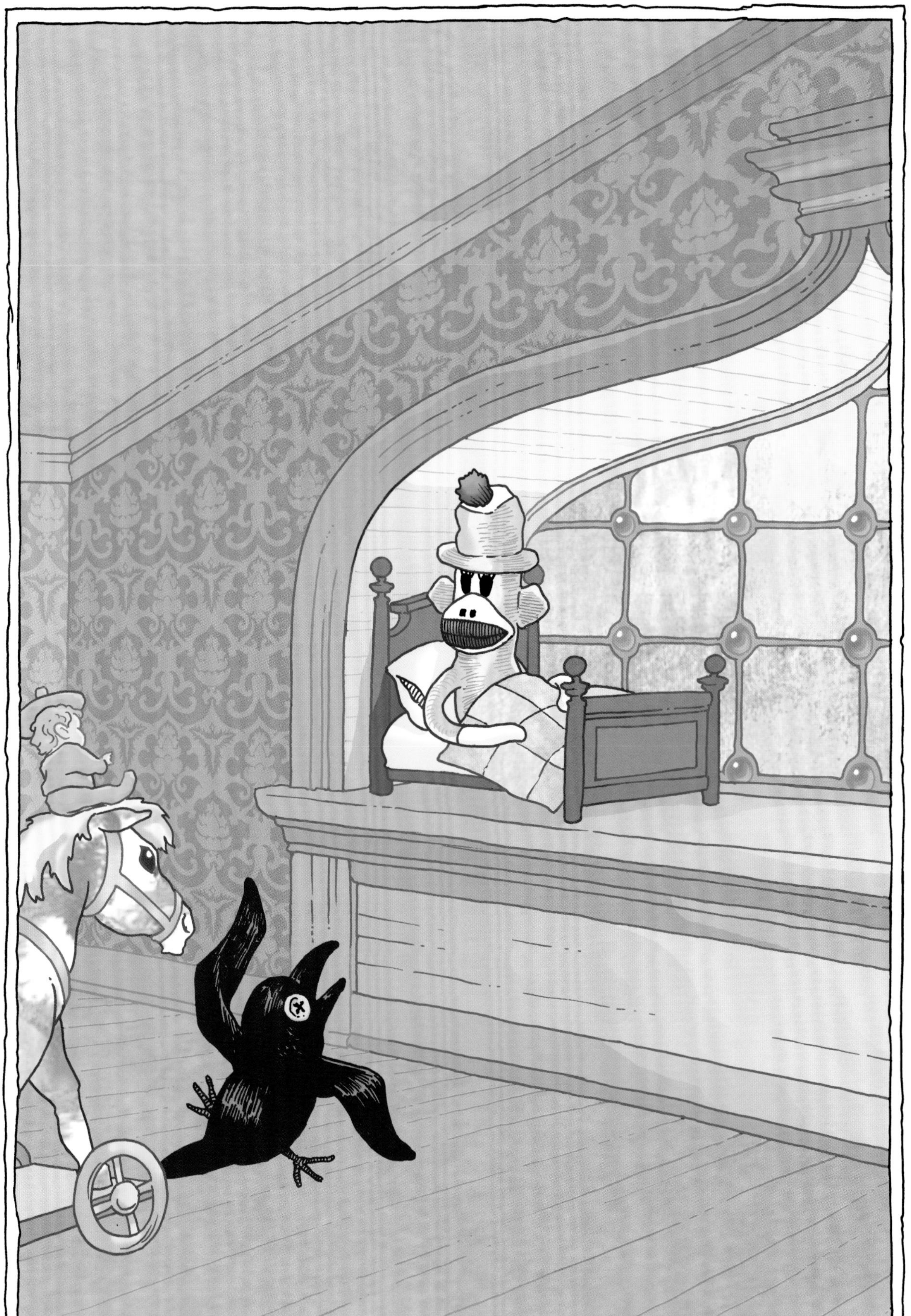

SO they all rode Stormy down the stairs.

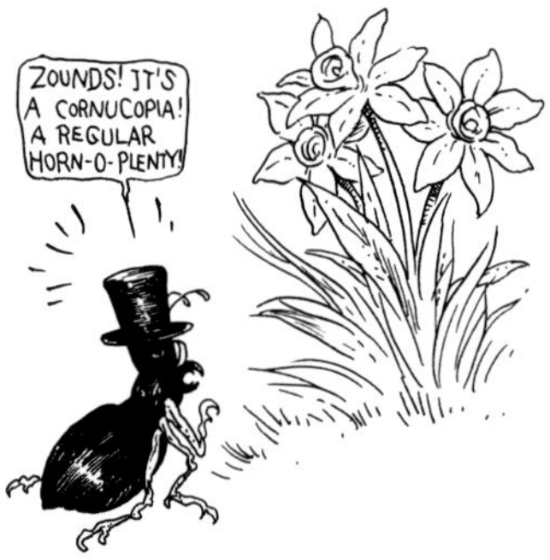
ZOUNDS! IT'S A CORNUCOPIA! A REGULAR HORN-O-PLENTY!

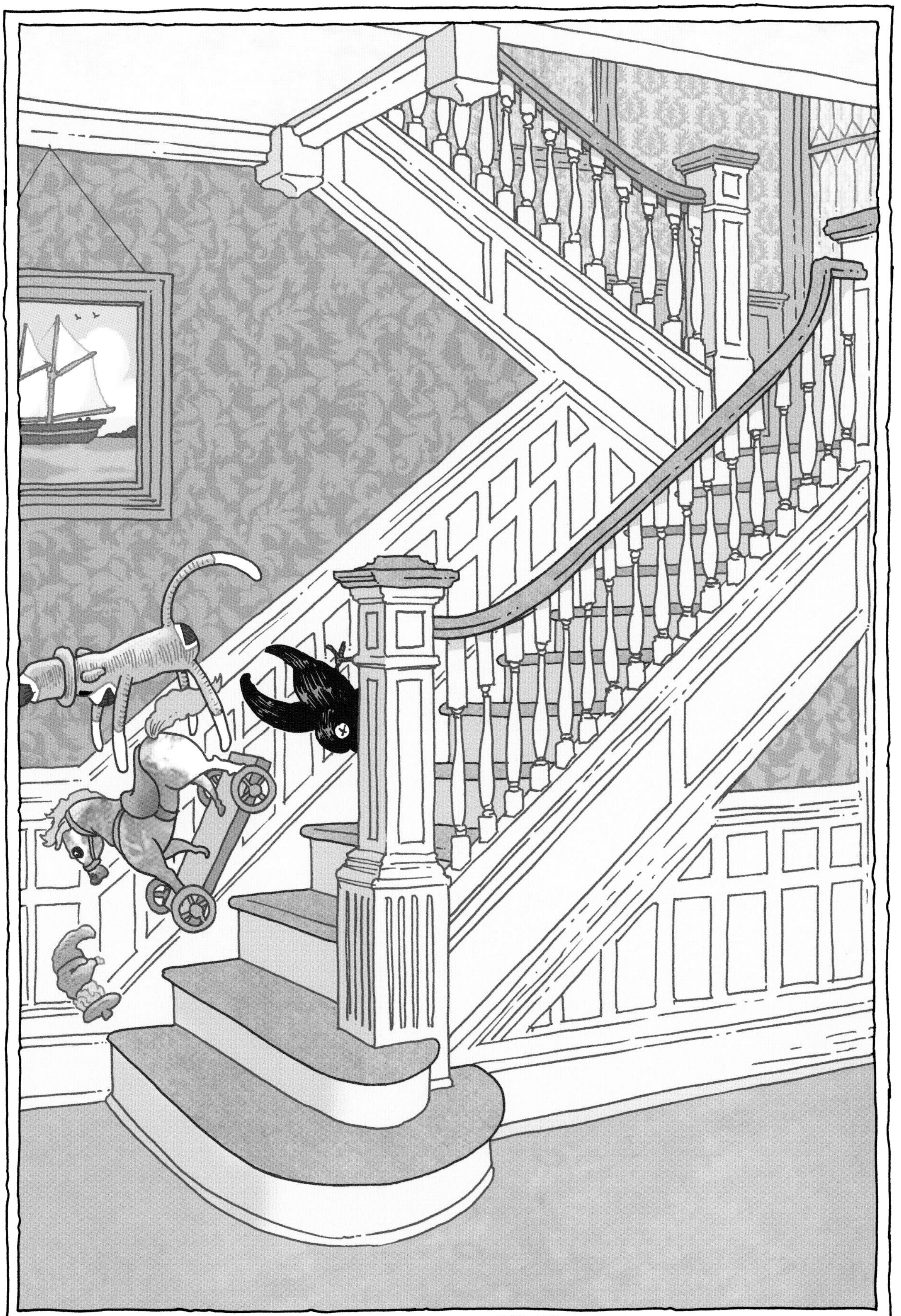

"LOOK at this!" cried Inches. "Isn't it fine?" She frolicked and jumped.

"Oh my, it's lovely!" the Sock Monkey said. "What is it?"

"It's some kind of spectrum--," began the crow, but Inches turned a somersault and interrupted, "I don't know what it is, but it's coming from that doorknob!"

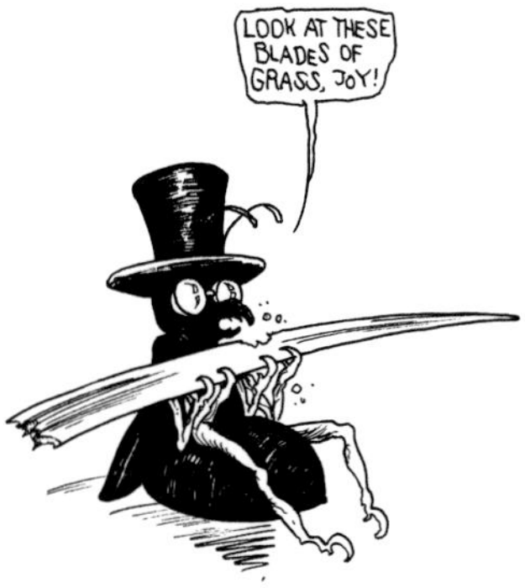
LOOK AT THESE BLADES OF GRASS, JOY!

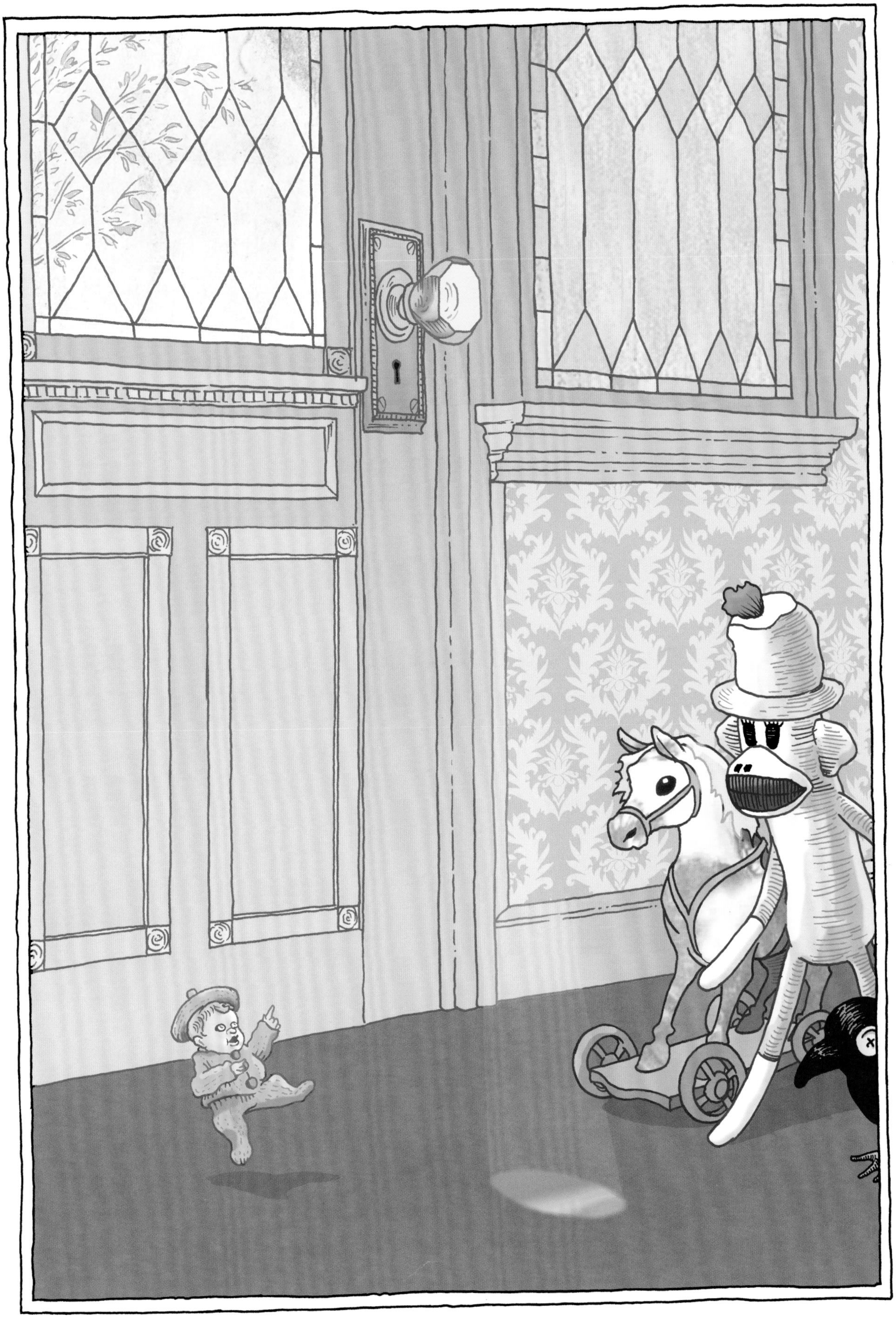

THAT night, the Sock Monkey couldn't sleep. "Isn't it grand," he thought, "to live in a world full of such beautiful things? Magical glass doorknobs, think of it!"

THE THISTLE SEED IS PURE AMBROSIA!

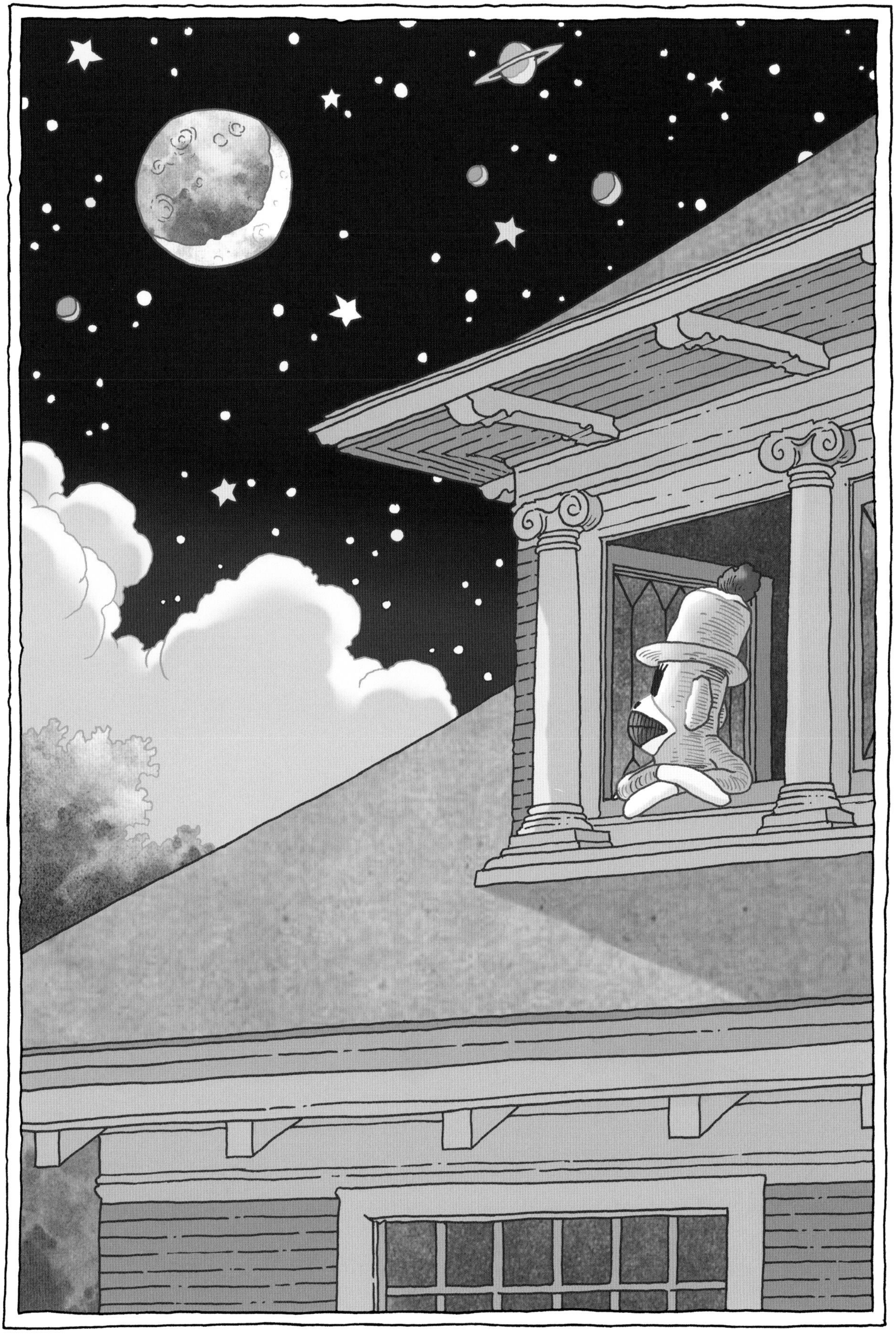

MEANWHILE, Mother
Nature was working some magic,
too, and the next morning there
were big summery leaves on all
the trees around the house.

HAVE YOU TRIED THESE ACORNS? THEY REALLY ARE SPECTACULAR!

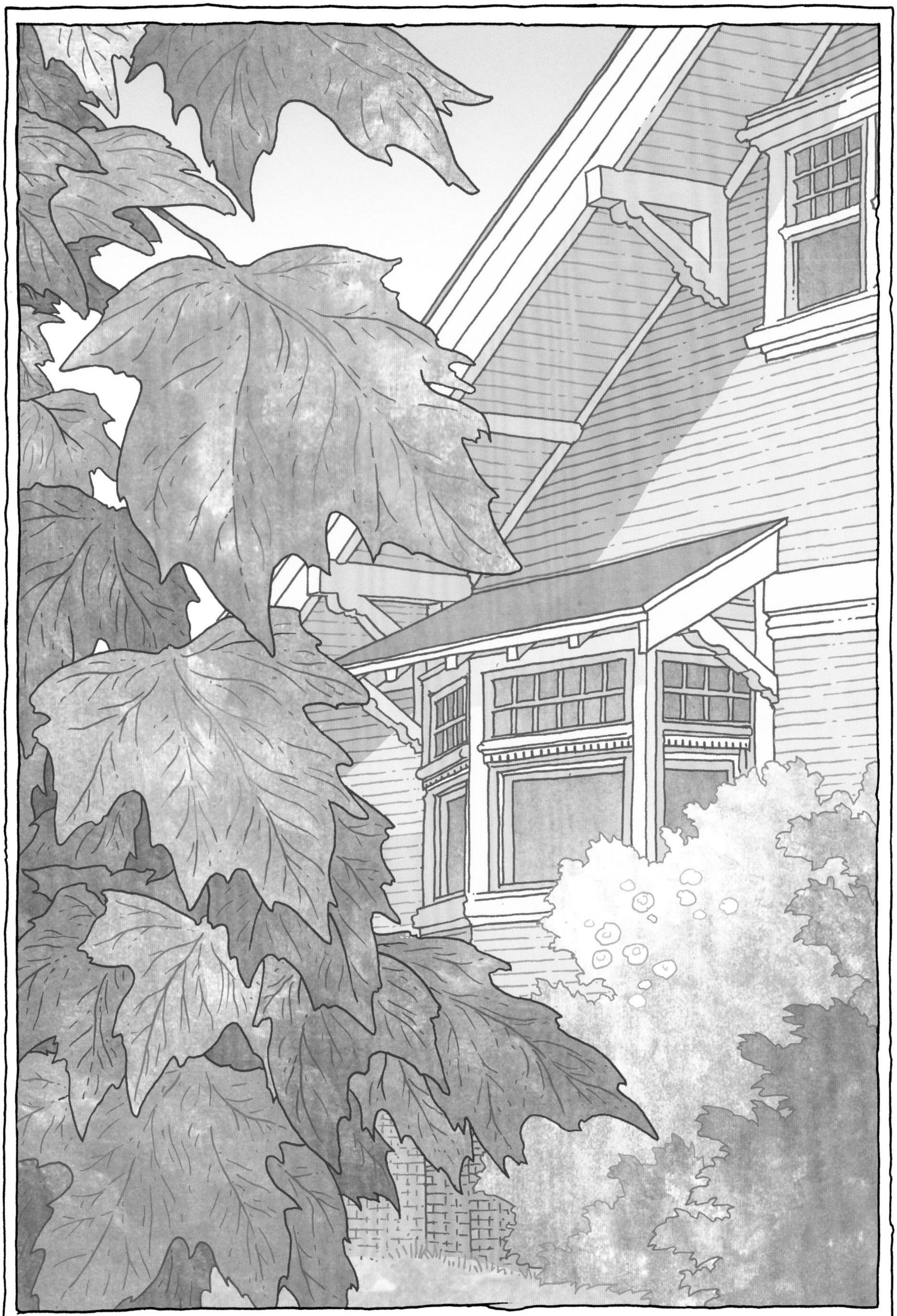

THE Sock Monkey tumbled downstairs, but when he got there, there was nothing to see! "It's broken!" he gasped.

WELL, I'VE NEVER EATEN AN ACORN BEFORE, IT SEEMED LIKE A SQUIRRELLY THING TO DO! BUT YOU'RE RIGHT, THEY ARE MAGNIFICENT!

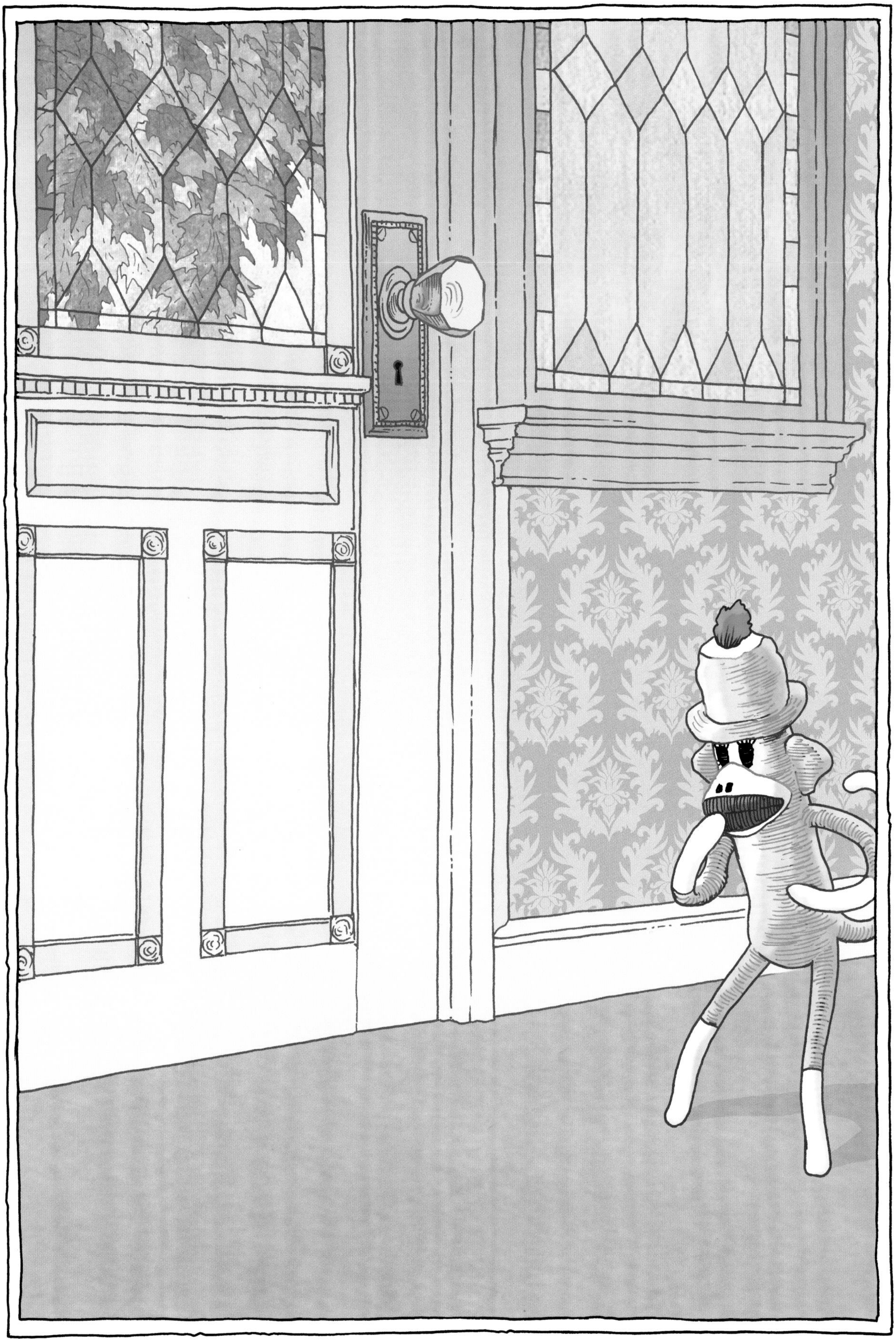

INCHES peered into the
doorknob. "It seems to have lost
its oomph!"

"This is scary," whispered Stormy,
"I'm getting skittish!"

"Hmmm..." The Sock Monkey had
an idea. "I think we can fix it."

OH, THE
DANDELIONS!
IF I HAD
A TOOTH,
I WOULD
CALL THEM
TOOTHSOME!

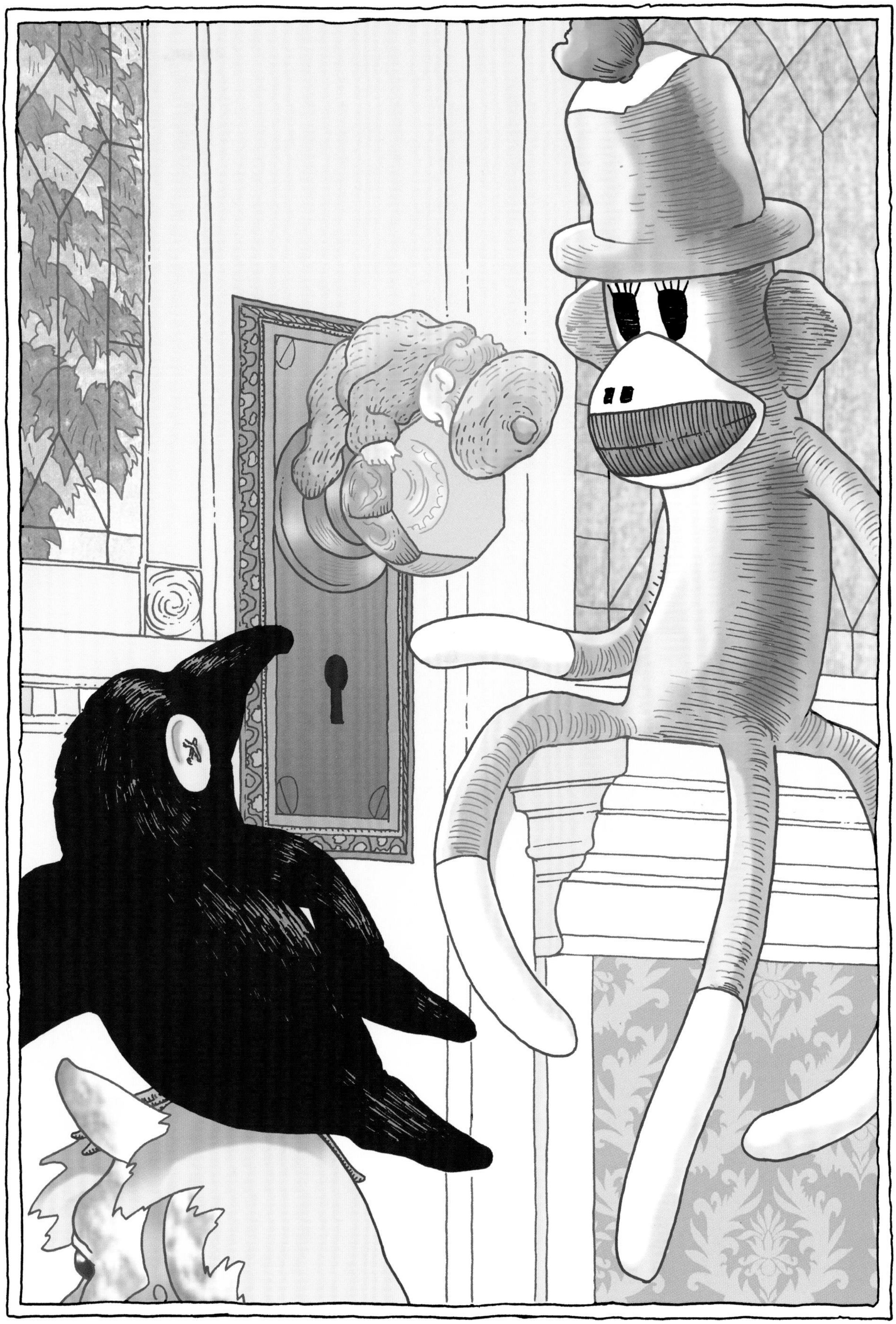

"WE'LL go around the house and collect all the shiny glass and crystal we can find. Maybe we can boost that doorknob's power!"

SCURVY, WHY IS IT THAT SOMETIMES THERE IS TOO MUCH TO EAT AND SOMETIMES THERE IS NOTHING?

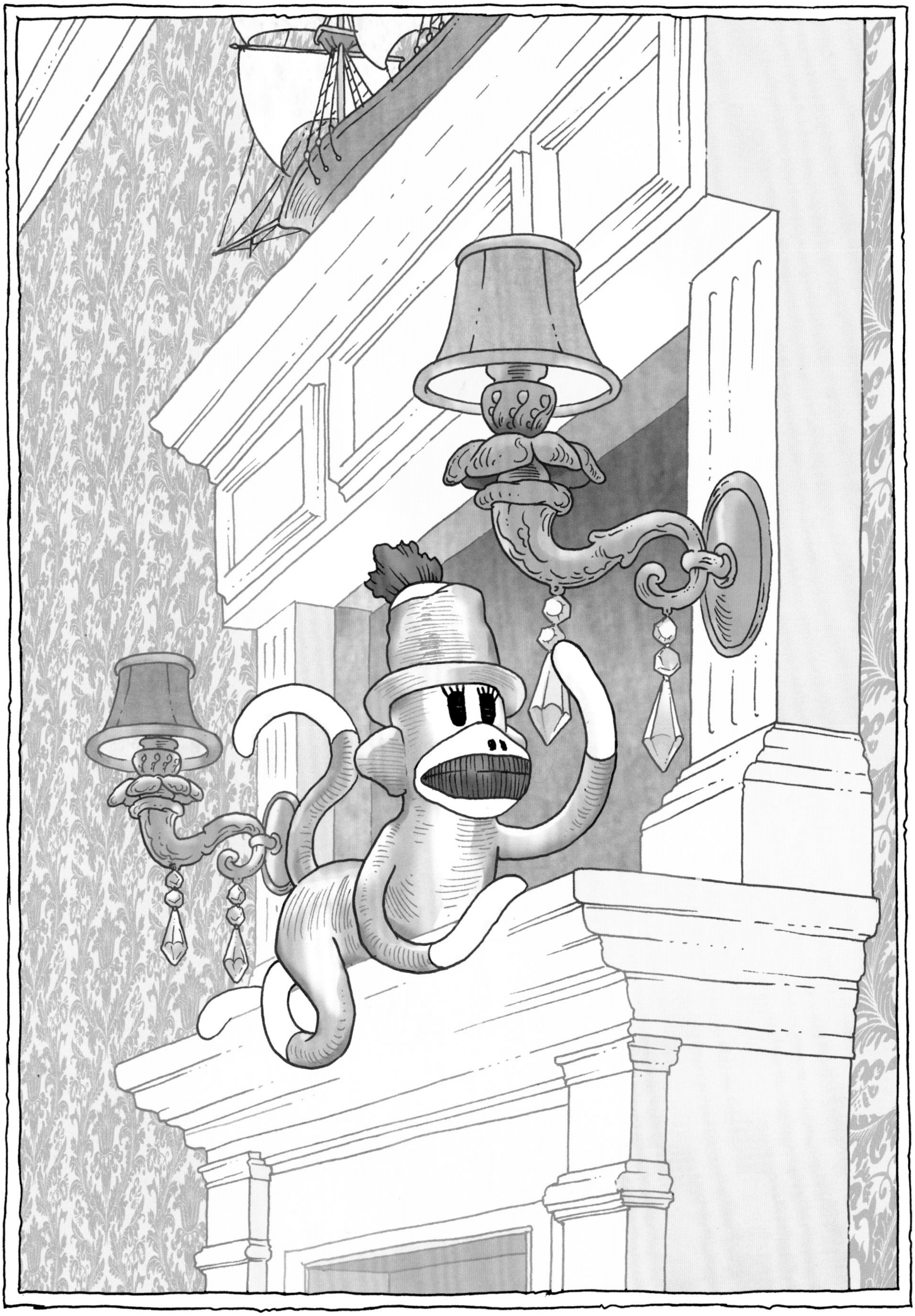

"HOW about this candy
dish?" asked the crow.

"Don't drop it, it will break for sure,"
replied the Sock Monkey as he stood
teetering on Stormy's back.

"Please hurry!" groaned Stormy.
"My wheels hurt!"

IT HAS TO DO WITH
FLUCTUATIONS IN
THE SEASON,
IF YOU SEE
WHAT I MEAN
RICKETS...

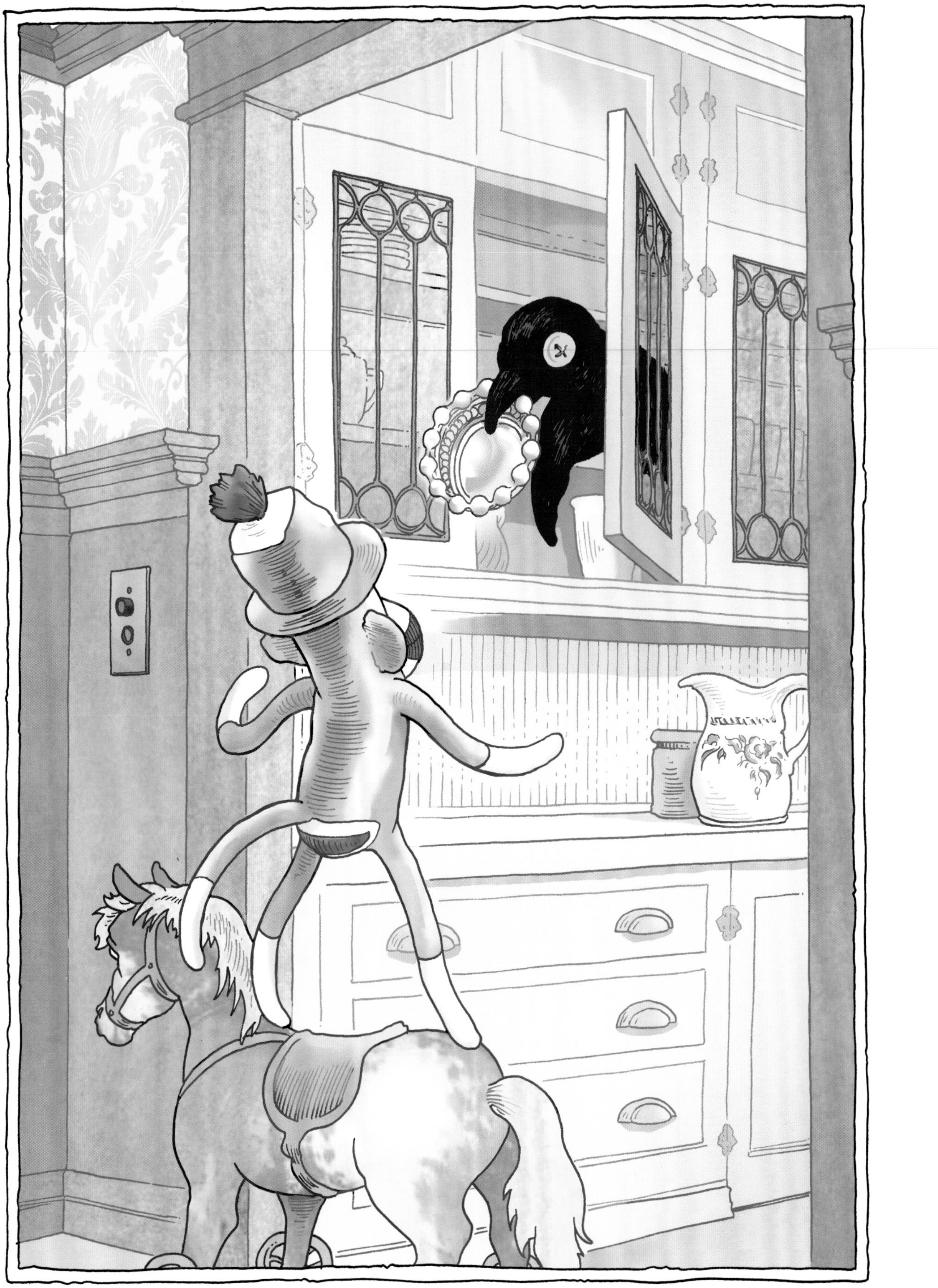

STORMY found a fine kaleidoscope, "I hope this helps."

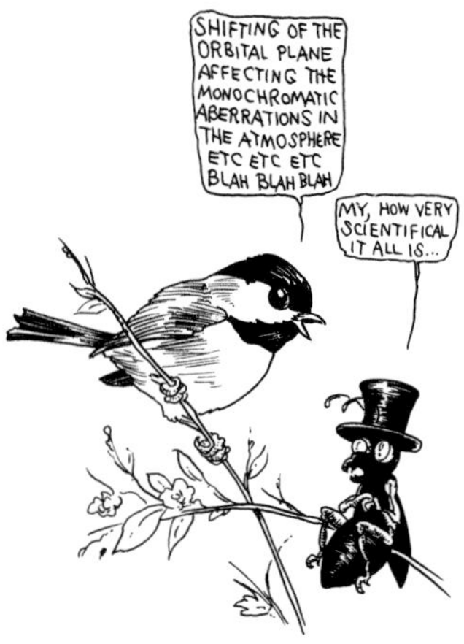
SHIFTING OF THE ORBITAL PLANE AFFECTING THE MONOCHROMATIC ABERRATIONS IN THE ATMOSPHERE ETC ETC ETC BLAH BLAH BLAH
MY, HOW VERY SCIENTIFICAL IT ALL IS...

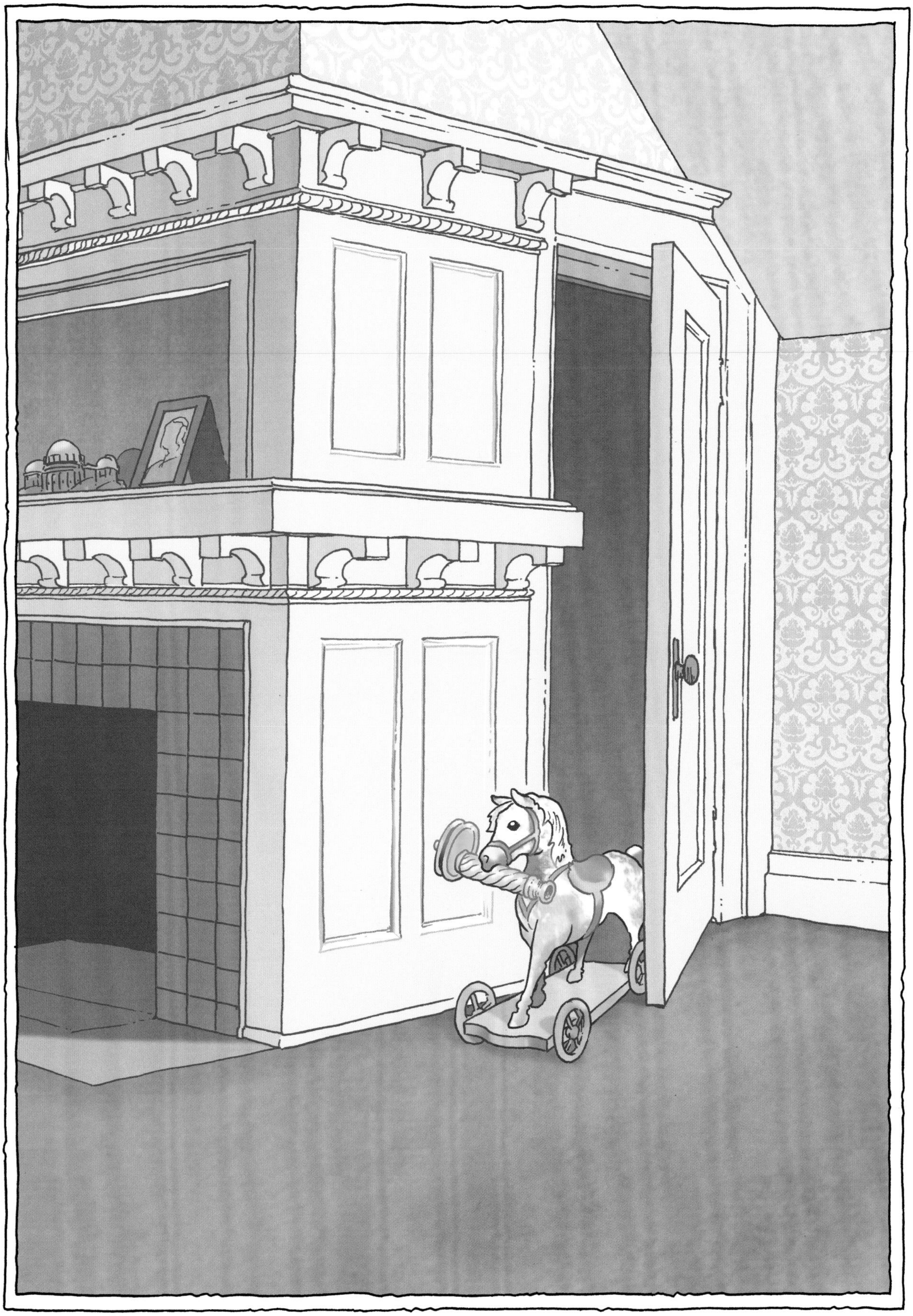

INCHES pulled out a magnifying glass, “If this doesn’t do the trick, nothing will!”

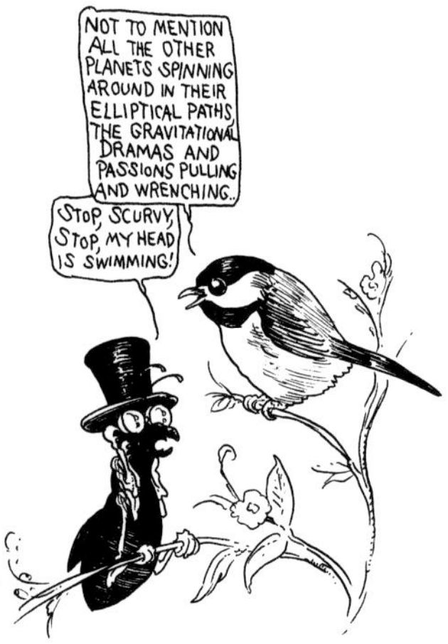
NOT TO MENTION ALL THE OTHER PLANETS SPINNING AROUND IN THEIR ELLIPTICAL PATHS THE GRAVITATIONAL DRAMAS AND PASSIONS PULLING AND WRENCHING..
STOP, SCURVY, STOP, MY HEAD IS SWIMMING!

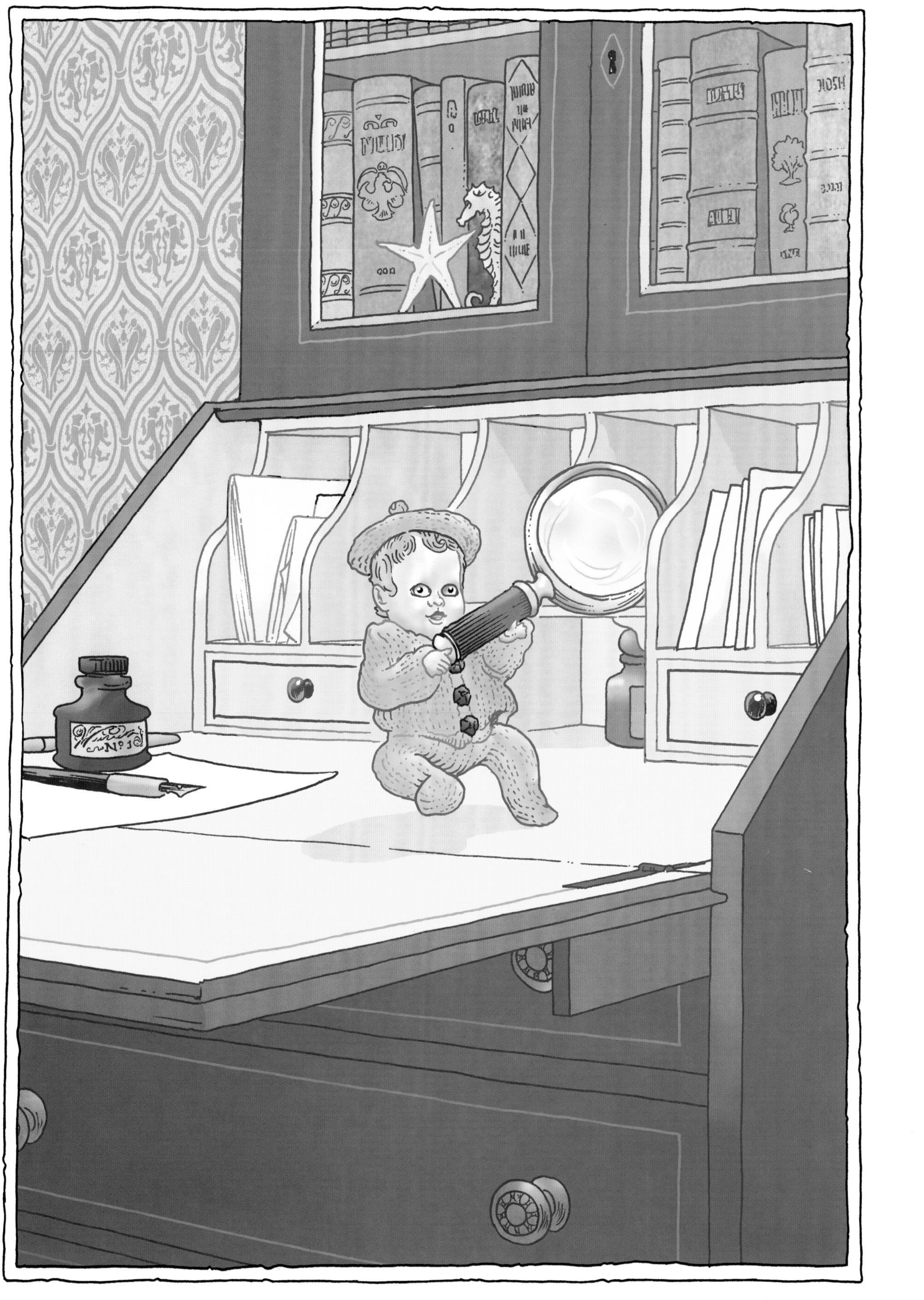

SITTING on the dressing
table, the Sock Monkey eyed
the perfume bottle, "I don't
know, should we?"

"You take it, Inches, you're the
bravest," said the crow nervously.

"I'm not going to take it!"
she squealed. "It's Mommy's!"

THE LEAVES ARE
TURNING COLOR,
SCURVY, AND I
FEEL THE BITING
CHILL OF
APPROACHING
WINTER...

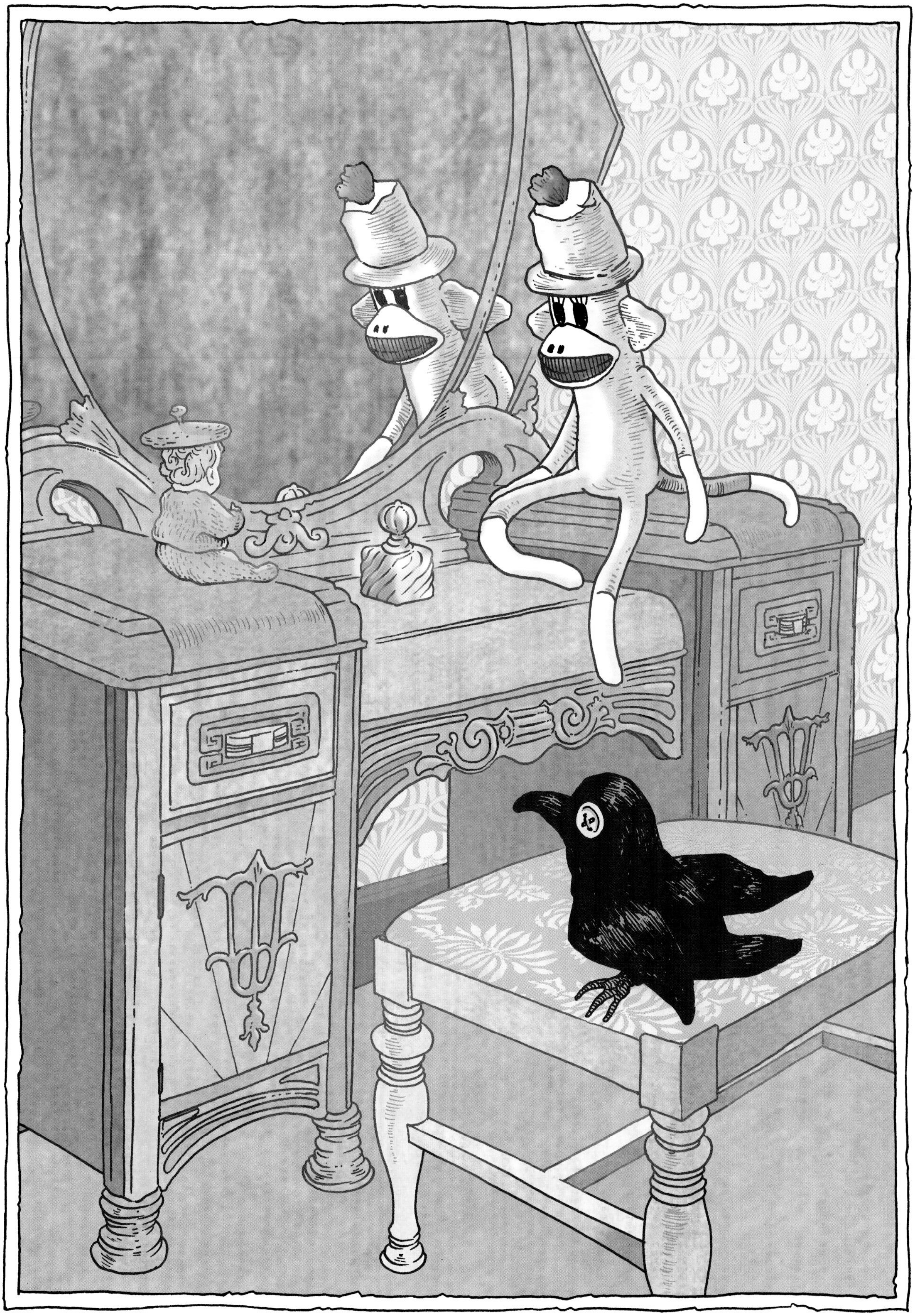

ALL summer long they worked, tying, taping, and tacking...

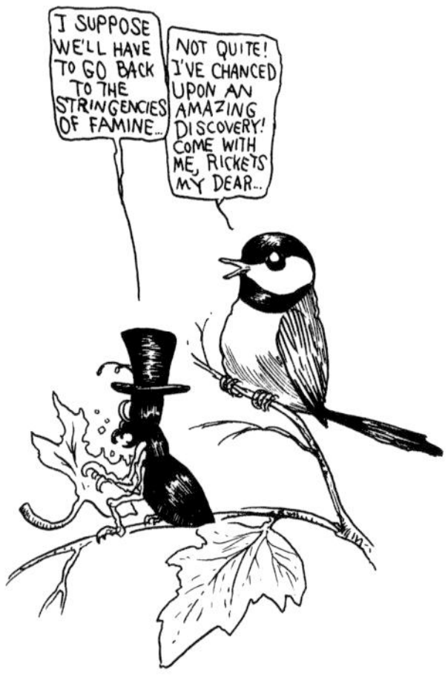
I SUPPOSE WE'LL HAVE TO GO BACK TO THE STRINGENCIES OF FAMINE...
NOT QUITE! I'VE CHANCED UPON AN AMAZING DISCOVERY! COME WITH ME, RICKETS MY DEAR...

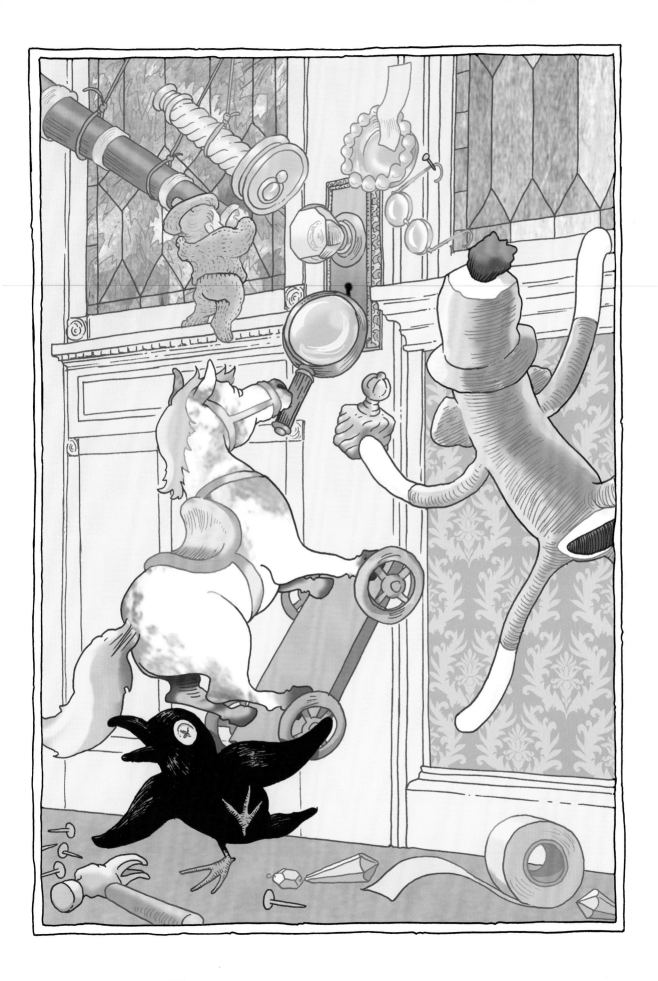

...but nothing helped.

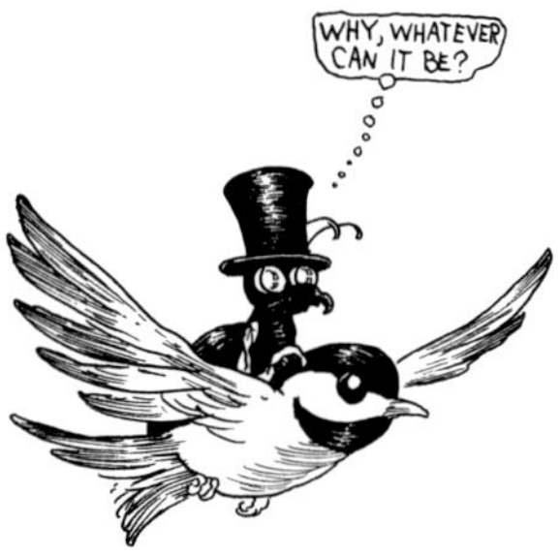
WHY, WHATEVER CAN IT BE?

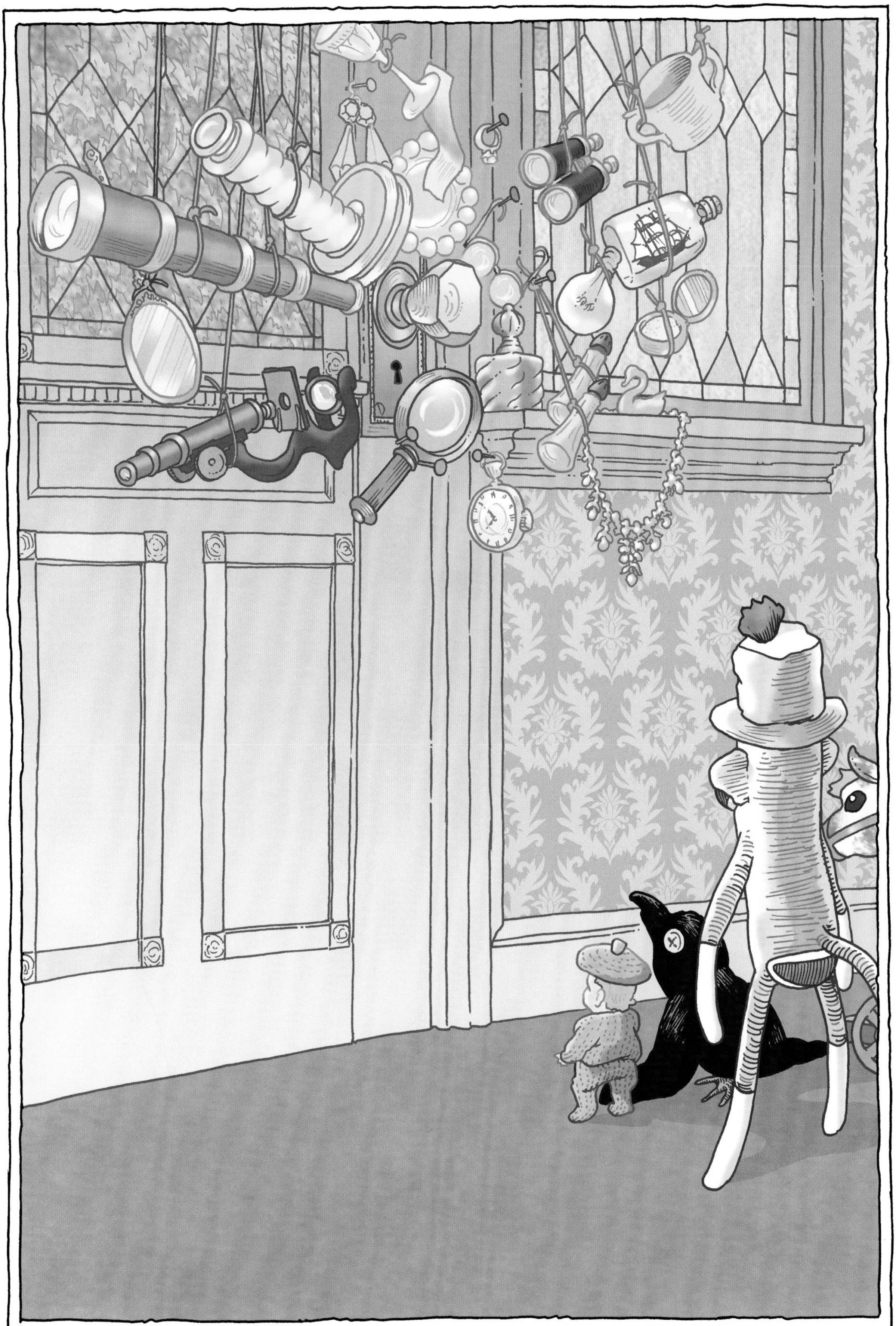

LATE one afternoon, a chilly autumn wind came and blew all the leaves off all the trees around the house. It blew all night! The next morning, the sun came shining through the window and...

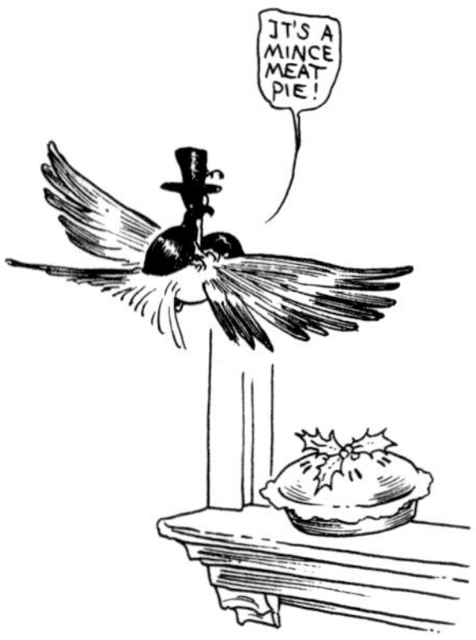
IT'S A MINCE MEAT PIE!

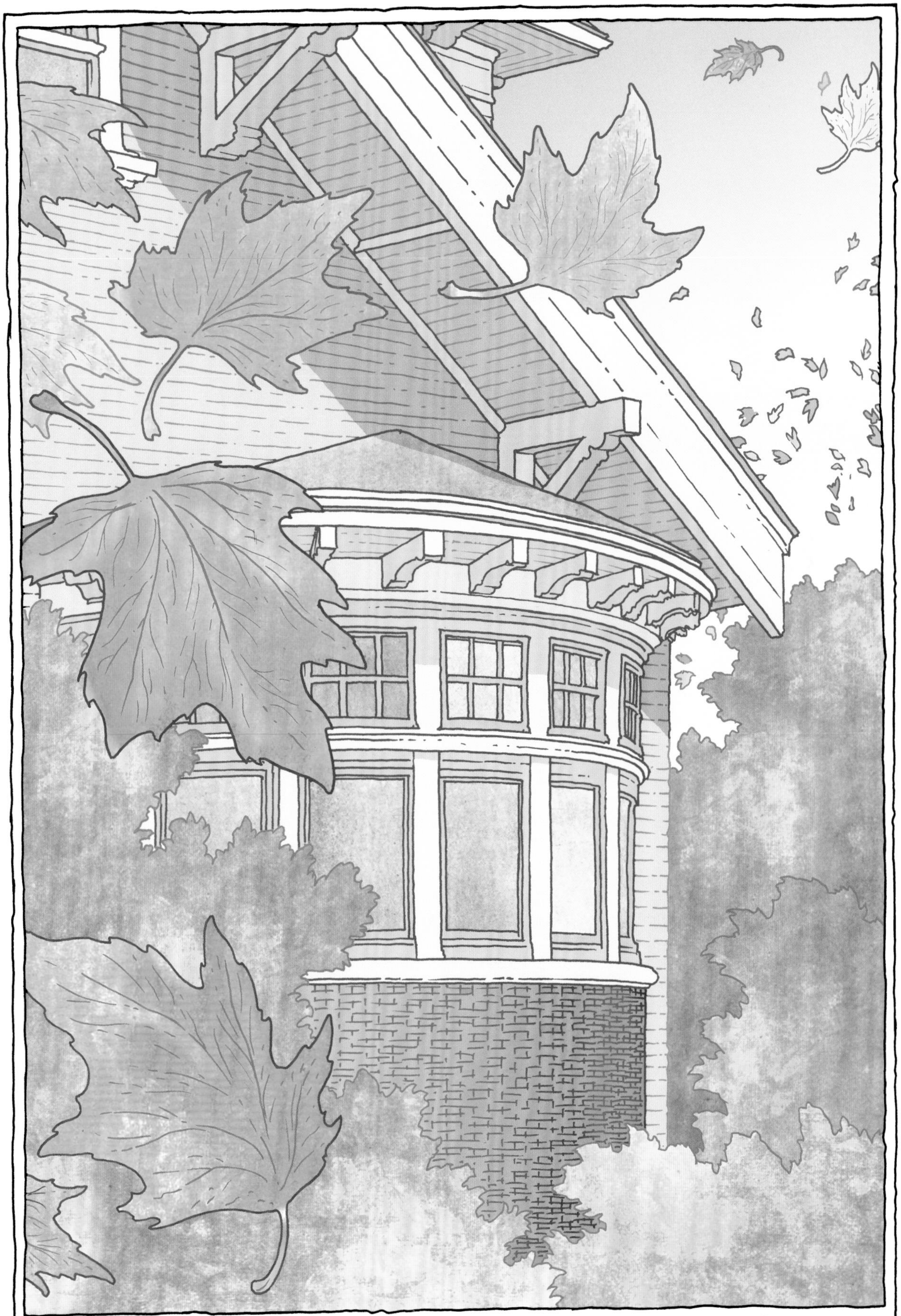

.........GADZOOKS!

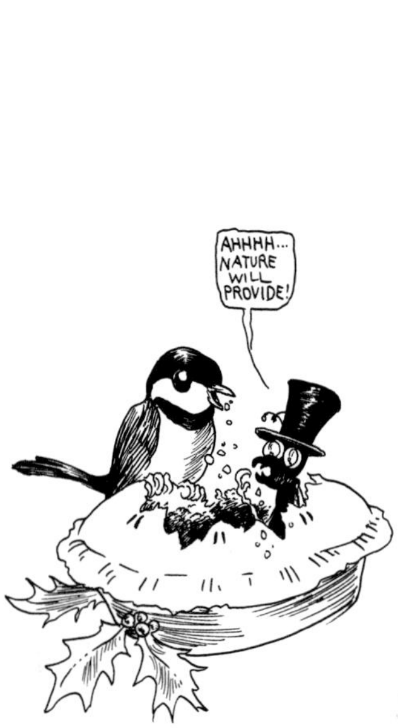
AHHHH...
NATURE
WILL
PROVIDE!

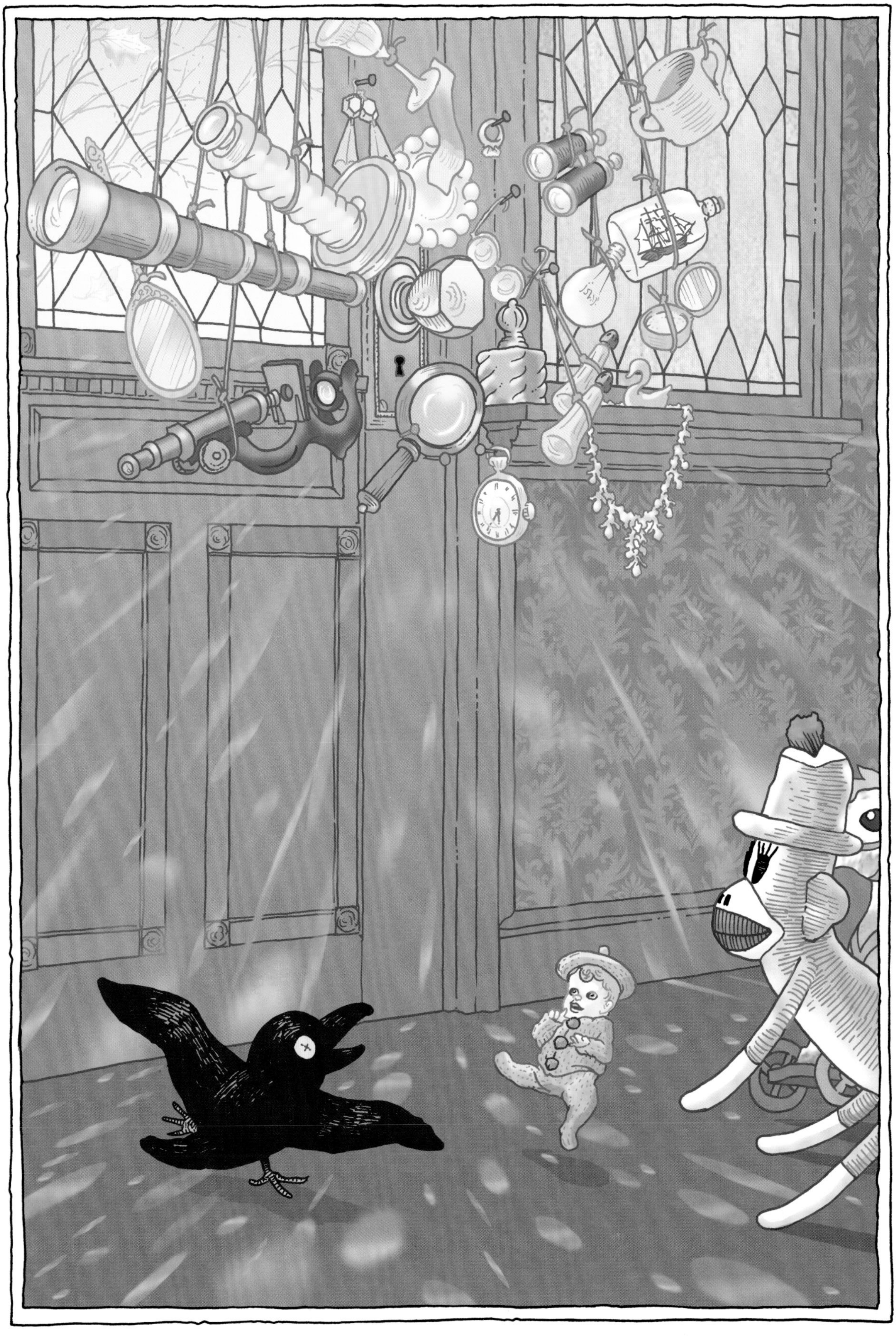